Nifty Knitting for Teens & Tweens

Learn to Knit Easy, Fun & Funky Knitting Projects Using Easy to Follow Instructions & Images

By

Helen Mao

Table of Contents

Introduction

Knitting is making a comeback these days with people looking for DIY activities, non-electronic hobbies, and ways to de-stress.

For multitaskers, what better way is there to keep your hands busy, make something, and be able to watch videos or chat with friends simultaneously? Of course, you don't have to do all those things at once if you don't want to!

Let's concentrate on knitting quick and handy projects for items you can wear, use yourself, or give as gifts.

This book describes ways to make simple knitting projects that appeal to all ages, especially tweens and teens - as I discovered with my daughters and their friends.

If you've already mastered the basic techniques of knitting (i.e., the knit stitch, the purl stitch, casting on, and casting off), then you are more than ready to tackle the projects described in this book.

These projects include:

- ❖ A pair of multi-colored hand warmers
- ❖ A phone cozy
- ❖ An infinity scarf
- ❖ A braided headband

With each of these projects, you'll build on your basic knitting knowledge. You will learn simple new techniques that make your finished product look advanced but actually are easy to execute.

Variety is the spice of life, and you'll be working with different weights of yarn and types of needles as well!

Any time you are unsure of a knitting term or technique, look it up on the internet: knitting websites and YouTube demonstrations can be incredibly helpful resources.

Don't be intimidated—all of these projects provide endless, effortless fun. Are you ready?

Chapter 1: Multicolored Hand Warmers

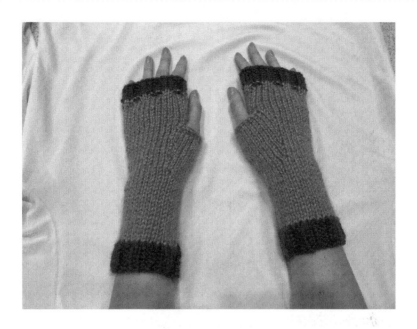

Do your hands ever feel slightly cold? Chilly enough for a little covering but not enough to pull on full gloves or thick mittens?

If so, try making these popular hand warmers. Cozy and convenient, they keep hands toasty while leaving fingers free to move and complete tasks unencumbered.

Get things done without sacrificing comfort! These hand warmers are perfect to wear while texting on the phone, typing at the computer, holding a book and turning pages while reading, practicing the piano, taking ballet class, etc.

With this project, you'll learn how to change yarn colors, execute a Make One (M1) stitch, and cast on stitches in the middle of a row.

Gather the following supplies:

- ❖ One skein (at most 5 ounces, 251 yards) of medium worsted weight (4) yarn in Color A for the piece's body. Acrylic, acrylic-wool blend, or wool is fine.
- ❖ A half skein of medium worsted weight (4) yarn in Color B (contrasting color) for the piece's ribbing
- ❖ One pair of size 8 straight knitting needles
- ❖ Two stitch markers
- ❖ One tapestry needle
- ❖ Row counter (optional)

This one-size-fits-all pattern is suitable for the average teen/adult. Feel free to adjust it (length-wise, width-wise) if you wish.

Each hand warmer's finished circumference at the upper and lower edges is about seven inches. The finished length from the top edge to the bottom edge is about nine and a half inches.

Be sure to check your gauge. The gauge for this pattern is 18 stitches by 16 rows equaling about four square inches in stockinette stitch.

If you end up needing to knit fewer stitches and rows to make a four-inch square, try using smaller size needles. If you end up needing to knit more stitches and rows to make a four-inch square, try using a larger size needle

This pattern can be used for both the left-hand and right-hand fingerless mittens. However, if you want the side seam to be positioned under each hand when you wear the finished mitten, then use these directions for the hand/thumb gusset section of the left-hand warmer:

Step 1: Cast on 28 stitches in Color B.

Step 2: Create the bottom ribbing by working in K2, P2 (rib stitch) for 6 rows (about one inch).

Step 3: Change Yarn Colors: change to Color A yarn.

Hold the finished ribbing as if you are going to knit your next row.

Instead of continuing to use Color B yarn, however, take Color A yarn and wrap it around the right needle a few times to prevent it from slipping off easily.

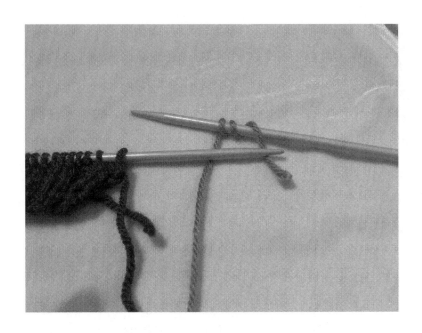

Start knitting with the right needle but use Color A yarn, not Color B yarn.

As you pull the loop of Color A through, don't pull it too hard as you may end up pulling Color A yarn off the right needle.

Tip: Hold onto the "tails" of both Colors A and B as while knitting the first few stitches in Color A.

Complete the first knit stitch in Color A–it becomes the first stitch on the right needle.

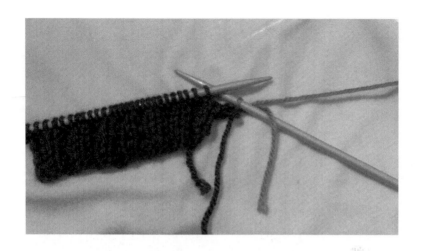

Repeat steps 2 and 3 to knit the second stitch in Color A.

Repeat steps 2 and 3 to knit a few more stitches. Tie the "tails" of Colors A and B into a knot to anchor Color A.

Cut the "tail" of Color B to free it from its skein; you are now working from the skein of Color A.

Step 4: Finish knitting the row in Color A and enjoy the contrasting colors!

Step 5: Then create the hand warmer's lower half, the section that covers the wrist by working in stockinette stitch for about three inches (another 17 rows).

Step 6: Now, you're ready to create the hand/thumb gusset section.

Row 1: K1, PM (place a marker on the needle). This is the mitten's right side (RS: knit/out-facing).

Execute M1 (make one stitch)

Add or increase by one knit stitch by lifting the horizontal thread lying between needles from the back with the right needle.

Then place the stitch onto the left needle and use the
right needle to knit a new stitch through the back loop.

Voilà–you have made (added/increased by) one new stitch on the right needle, just left of the marker.

Then K6, M1, and PM (place the second marker on the needle).

Then knit to the end of the row. You've now increased or added two new stitches.

<u>Rows 2-4</u>: Continue in stockinette stitch.

<u>Row 5</u>: K1, slip marker (SM), M1, knit to next marker, M1, SM, knit to the end of the row. You've increased or added two new stitches.

<u>Rows 6-8</u>: Continue in stockinette stitch.

<u>Row 9</u>: repeat Row 5. You've increased or added two new stitches.

<u>Rows 10-12</u>: Continue in stockinette stitch.

<u>Row 13</u>: repeat Row 5. You've increased or added two new stitches.

<u>Row 14</u>: Purl to marker, remove marker, P2, bind off 10 stitches for thumb opening, P2, remove marker, and purl to end of row.

<u>Row 15</u>: Knit to the bound-off stitches.

Cast On in the Middle of This Row: here are instructions for how to cast on 2 stitches over the bound-off stitches.

Turn over the work, so the purl side (wrong side: WS) is facing up.

Bring yarn between needles to back.

Insert right needle through the front (from left to right) of the end stitch on the left needle.

Wind the yarn around, behind, and then over the right needle.

Use the right needle to pull through the loop.

Use the right needle to pull the loop off the left needle but keep the end stitch on the left needle.

Insert the left needle under the loop (from right front) on the right needle.

Slide the left needle through the loop, remove the right needle from the loop and voilà - you've cast on 1 stitch in the middle of a row.

Repeat the above steps in order to cast on the second stitch in the middle of this row.

Then turn the work back over again, so RS is facing up.

Continue to knit to the end of the row, closing the hole you've just created for the thumb.

Knit to the end of this row.

Step 7: Knit in stockinette stitch for about one and a half inches (9 rows).

Step 8: To create the top ribbing, change back to yarn Color B and K2, P2 (rib stitch) for the next 6 rows, about one inch.

Step 5: Cast off stitches loosely in rib stitch.

For the hand/thumb gusset section of the _right-hand warmer_:

Step 1: Cast on 28 stitches in Color B.

Step 2: Create the bottom ribbing by working in K2, P2 (rib stitch) for 6 rows (about one inch).

Step 3: Change to Color A yarn and knit 1 row.

Continue creating the hand warmer's lower half (i.e., the section that covers the wrist) by working in stockinette stitch for about three inches (another 17 rows).

Step 4: Create the hand/thumb gusset section.

<u>Row 1</u>: K21, PM, M1, K6, M1, PM, K1.

Since the beginning, you have increased or added two new stitches, bringing the total number of stitches in this row to 30.

<u>Rows 2-4</u>: Continue in stockinette stitch.

Row 5: K1 to marker, SM, M1, knit to next marker, M1, SM, knit to the end of the row. You've increased or added two new stitches.

Rows 6-8: Continue in stockinette stitch.

Row 9: repeat Row 5. You've increased or added two new stitches.

Rows 10-12: Continue in stockinette stitch.

Row 13: repeat Row 5. You've increased or added two new stitches.

Row 14: (WS) Purl to marker, remove marker, P2, bind off 10 stitches for thumb opening, P2, remove marker, and purl to end of row.

Row 15: (RS) Knit, casting on 2 stitches over bound-off stitches. You've increased or added two new stitches.

Step 5: Knit in stockinette stitch for about one and a half inches (9 rows).

Step 6: To create the top ribbing, change back to Color B yarn and K2, P2 (rib stitch) for the next 6 rows, about one inch.

Step 7: Cast off stitches loosely in rib stitch. Now you have finished hand warmer pieces.

Step 8: Fold the finished piece in half lengthwise, wrong side to the wrong side. Use a tapestry needle to sew the side seam.

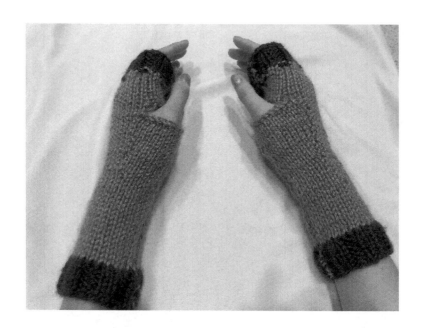

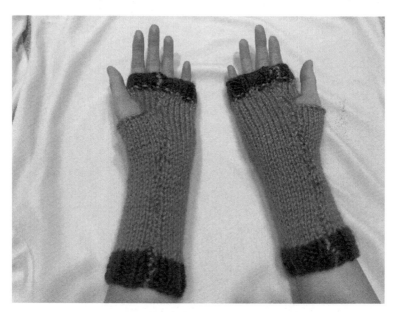

Customize the hand warmers as you wish.

You may lengthen the wrist section for more coverage, shorten the wrist section for less coverage, cast on more stitches to widen, or fewer stitches to make narrower in multiples of four.

All the while, still follow the basic pattern shape.

In this next chapter, we'll create a cover for your phone.

Chapter 2: Basket Weave Phone Cozy

Since nearly everyone has a cell phone nowadays, this practical and quick project can be used by anyone.

Although many people protect their cell phones with cases, this basket weave phone cozy adds a soft touch and can prevent screens and cases (or naked phones) from getting scratched.

Here's an idea: actually put your phone away, but not too far away or buried in a bag.

Put it in the basket weave phone cozy to keep it from becoming a distraction while still easily accessible.

With this project, you'll learn how to use double pointed needles (DPN) to knit in the round and to join end stitches in the round.

Gather the following supplies:

- ❖ 10g of double knitting (DK)/lightweight (3) yarn
- ❖ four size 6 (4mm) double pointed needles
- ❖ one stitch marker
- ❖ one tapestry needle
- ❖ needle point protectors/stoppers (optional)
- ❖ row counter (optional)

DPN are often used for knitting in the round for seamless cylindrical items with small circumferences and diameters, such as socks or leg warmers.

Working with DPN isn't difficult, but because both ends of each are pointed, stitches can slip off easily. Therefore, knitters new to DPN might want to try DPN made from wood, which is less slippery than metal or plastic needles.

Needle point protectors–which look like mini rubber cones–are meant to protect the ends of needles, keep them sharp, and prevent them from poking other objects.

They also stop stitches from sliding off (which protects my sanity, keeps me happy, and prevents me from stabbing other objects in frustration).

Although gauge is important is most knitting projects, it isn't really crucial for this project. This pattern can fit loosely over an iPhone 8 with a thin case or fits snugly over an iPhone 10R with an OtterBox case.

Step 1: Cast on 32 stitches on one needle.

Step 2: Transfer 22 stitches onto a second needle, slipping the stitches as if to purl.

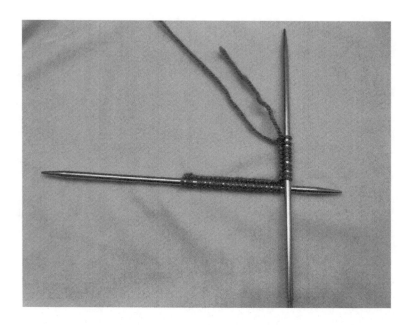

Step 3: Transfer 11 stitches from the second needle onto the third needle. Position the three needles in a U shape.

You should have 10 stitches on the first needle (right side of the U), 11 stitches on the second needle (bottom of U), and 11 stitches on the third needle (left side of the U).

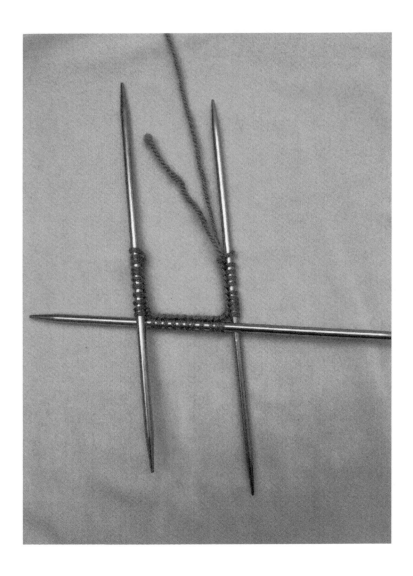

Step 4: Join end stitches in the round.

Position the three needles into a triangle.

Insert the right needle in front of and under the end stitch on the left needle.

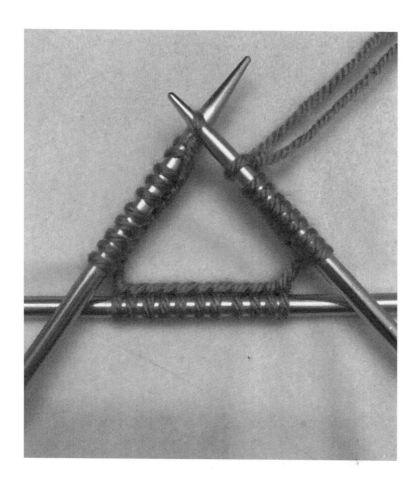

Slip the end stitch off the left needle and onto the right needle.

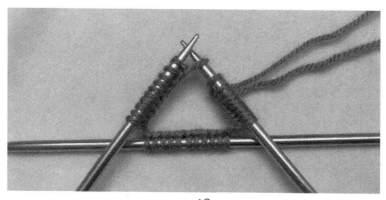

Insert the left needle in front of and under the next-to-end stitch (what used to be the end stitch) on the right needle.

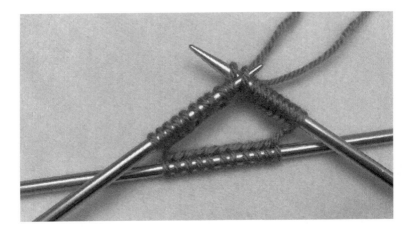

With the left needle, lift the second stitch over the slipped stitch and off the right needle; now the stitch is on the left needle.

The two slipped stitches should cross each other.

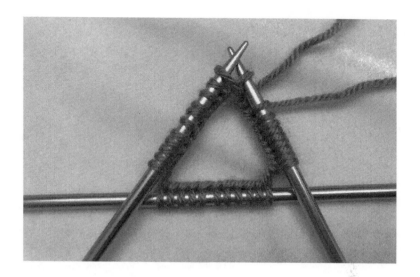

Step 5: Use the fourth DPN to begin knitting in the round.

At the beginning of a round (row), knit 1 stitch, PM, and then knit the rest of the row.

Once you've completed one row, you'll know that your next row begins when there is one stitch left before the stitch marker.

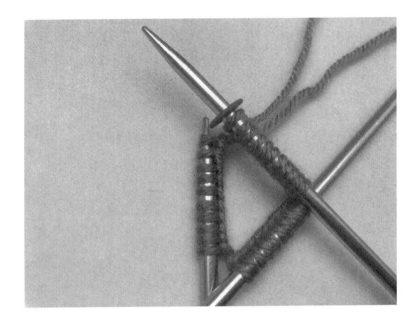

As you knit, you'll be transferring stitches from one needle to another, thus freeing up one needle each time you finish one needle.

Use the free needle to knit the next needle.

Tip: If you want to use a counter to keep track of what row you are on, put a round counter on the end of one of the needles, or use a hand counter.

Step 6: Follow this pattern.

<u>Row 1</u>: Knit

Row 2: (P5, K3) four times

Row 3: (P5, K3) four times

Row 4: (P5, K3) four times

<u>Row 5</u>: Knit

<u>Row 6</u>: (P1, K3, P5, K3, P4) two times

<u>Row 7</u>: (P1, K3, P5, K3, P4) two times

<u>Row 8</u>: (P1, K3, P5, K3, P4) two times

Step 7: Repeat Rows 1 through 8 five more times or until the case fits over your phone with an inch to go.

Step 8: End in a knit row.

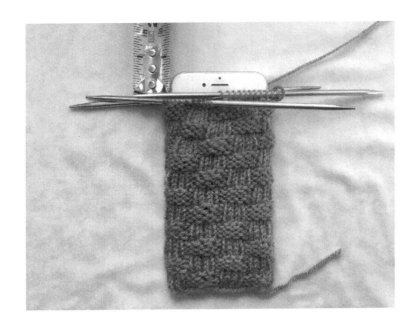

Step 9: Knit ribbing (K2, P2) until the case reaches the desired length past the end of your phone.

Step 10: Cast off stitches loosely in rib stitch.

Step 11: Use a tapestry needle to sew the bottom seam of the phone case.

51

Chapter 3: Double Moss Infinity Scarf

Infinity scarves are all the rage. They're stylish, convenient, and easy to wear without any ends to tuck in.

Infinity scarves look great on anyone at any age, but I noticed my daughters and friends knitting them quite often as their project of choice.

With this double moss infinity scarf project, you'll learn how to use a circular needle to knit in the round, join end stitches in the round, and knit the double moss stitch pattern.

Gather the following supplies:

- ❖ three skeins of bulky weight (5) yarn (about 300-400 yards)
- ❖ US 13 (9 mm) 29" circular needle
- ❖ one stitch marker
- ❖ row counter (optional)

As with DPN, circular needles are used for knitting in the round.

Unlike DPN, though, circular needles are one single neat piece: two needles joined by a cord for holding stitches.

Also, stitches are not as likely to easily slip off circular needles.

Finally, while DPN are used for knitting small circular items (like socks), circular needles can accommodate larger projects.

Circular needles come in varying lengths, from nine inches (for baby hats) to 40+ inches (for larger flat projects like bed-size blankets).

Although gauge is important is most knitting projects, it isn't really as crucial for this project because this scarf is not anywhere near form-fitting.

A finished double moss infinity scarf measures about 11 inches wide with a circumference of 78 inches.

Step 1: Cast on 134 stitches.

Step 2: Join end stitches in the round.

Insert the right needle under end stitch on the left needle.

Slip end stitch off the left needle and onto the right needle.

Insert the left needle in front of and under the next-to-end stitch (what used to be the end stitch) on the right needle.

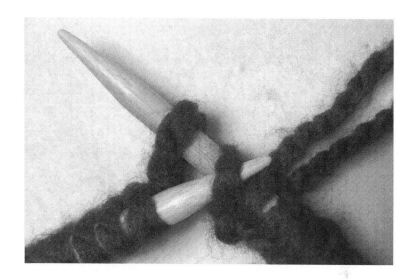

With the left needle, lift the second stitch over the slipped stitch and off the right needle; now the stitch is on the left needle. The two slipped stitches should cross each other.

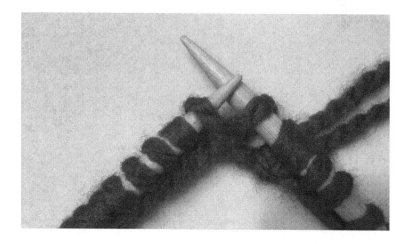

Step 3: Knit 1 stitch, place stitch marker (PM), and then knit the rest of the round (row).

Once you've completed one row, you'll know that your next row begins when there is one stitch left before the stitch marker.

Tip: If you want to use a counter to keep track of what row you are on, hang a counter from the stitch marker, or use a hand counter.

Step 4: Begin knitting pattern in the round.

Row 1: K2, P2 (repeat to end of the row)

<u>Row 2</u>: P2, K2 (repeat to end of the row)

The resulting pattern is a double moss stitch.

Step 5: Work until piece measures about 11 inches wide or as wide as you wish.

Step 6: Bind off loosely.

Wearing this double moss stitch infinity scarf in style is easy.

Loop it around your neck and straighten it out full length.

Twist it to make a second loop.

Pull the second loop over your head.

Chapter 4: Braided Cable Headband

Need to keep your head warm but don't want to wear a hat? Want a more stylish look than ear muffs?

Then try making and wearing this braided cable headband.

With this project, you'll learn how to knit a braided cable, which looks fancy but is pretty easy.

Gather the following supplies:

- ❖ one skein (about 100 grams, 87 yards) of super bulky weight (6) yarn
- ❖ one pair of size 10.5 straight knitting needles
- ❖ one cable needle (CN)–U-shaped (shown, but you can use another-shaped CN if you wish)
- ❖ one tapestry needle
- ❖ row counter

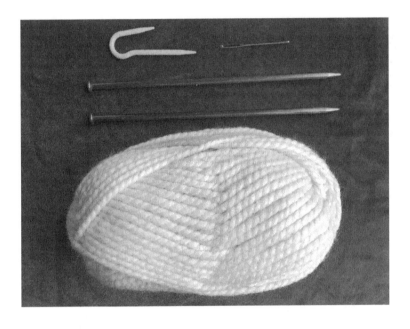

Step 1: Cast on 18 stitches.

Step 2: Follow this stitch pattern.

<u>Row 1</u>: K18

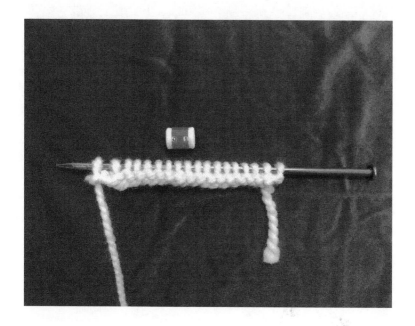

<u>Row 2</u>: K3, P12, K3

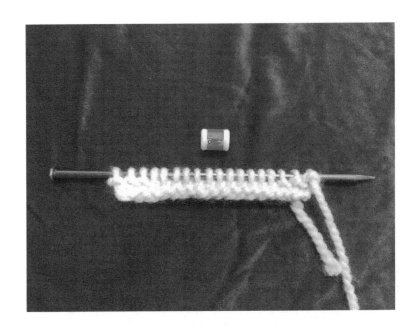

Row 3: Make front cable/cable twisting left.

K3, slip the next 4 stitches to the CN and hold in front

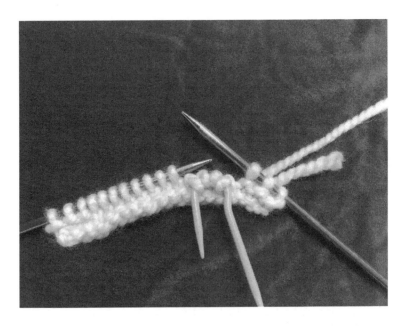

K4 from the left needle

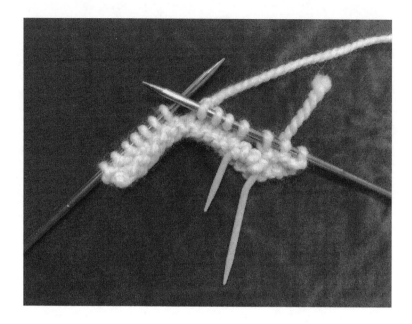

K4 from CN

K7

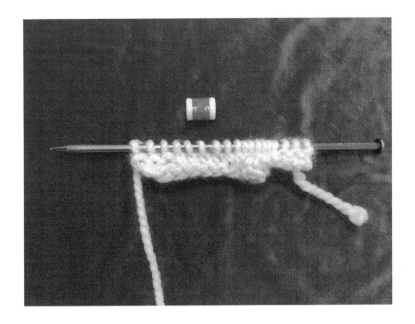

Row 4: K3, P12, K3

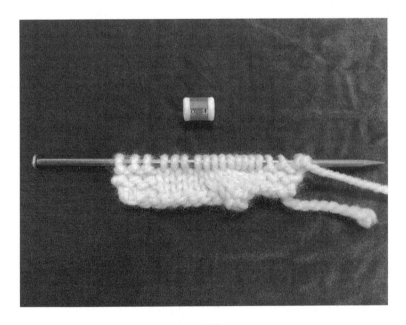

Row 5: K18

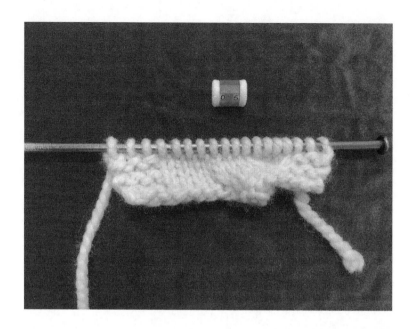

Row 6: K3, P12, K3

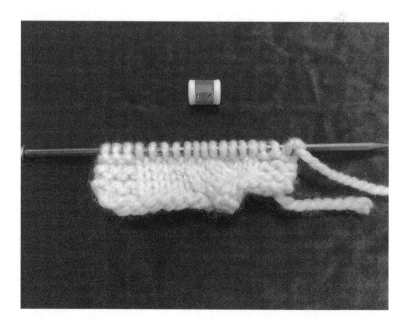

<u>Row 7</u>: Make back cable/cable twisting right.

K7, slip the next 4 stitches to the CN and hold in back

K4 from left needle

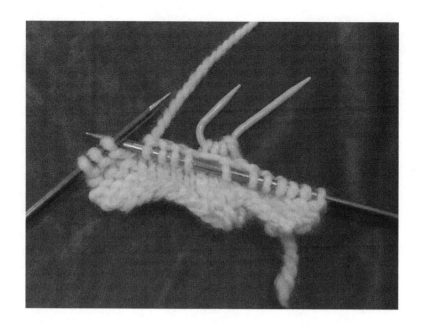

K4 from CN

K3

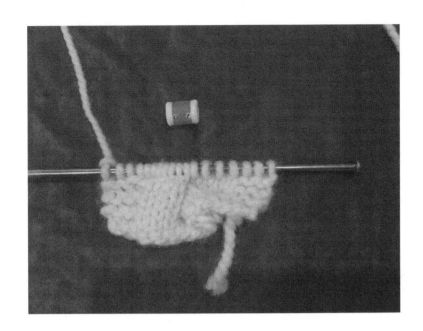

<u>Row 8</u>: K3, P12, K3

Step 3: Repeat Rows 1 through 8 eleven times or until the headband measures to the desired length.

It should be long enough to wrap around your head with a one-inch gap.

Tip: Purposely leave the headband a little short, so it is well fitted and stays on your head when you wear it; it stretches out.

Step 4: End on a row with K18, cast off loosely and sew the ends together.

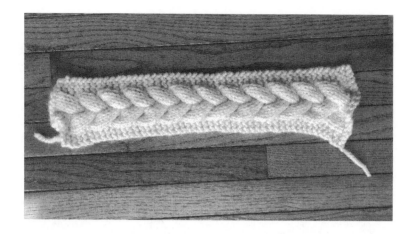

Step 5: Bind off and use a **tapestry needle** to sew the short ends together.

Conclusion

Congratulations! Pat yourself on the back because you've graduated beyond beginner knitting!

You've added more techniques to your "knitting toolbox." Just think about all the flexibility you now have!

You have now learned these advanced knitting techniques:

- ❖ Using double pointed needles (DPN) to knit in the round
- ❖ How to use a circular needle to knit in the round
- ❖ Using a cable needle
- ❖ How to change yarn colors in the middle of a project
- ❖ Increase or add a stitch through M1
- ❖ Cast on stitches in the middle of a row
- ❖ Knit a basket weave pattern
- ❖ Knit the Double Moss Stitch pattern
- ❖ Knit a braided cable
- ❖ Join end stitches in the round.

On top of that, you now have experience working with different weights of yarn, including:

- ❖ DK (double knitting) weight or lightweight (3)
- ❖ medium worsted weight (4)
- ❖ bulky weight (5)
- ❖ super bulky weight (6).

Finally, don't forget that you can customize any of these projects because you decide what type of yarn you want to us, as long as it's the weight required by the project's pattern.

Browse through yarns of different colors (bright, earth tone, pastel, mixed), fibers (acrylic, wool, cotton, combinations of these), and textures (regular, fuzzy, bouclé). Play around and experiment with various types of yarn to dress up or dress down any project.

Proudly put your personal touch on anything you knit because you have the freedom, creativity, and know-how. Enjoy knitting when chilling out or on the go. In the end, you'll have a cool finished product.

If this book of projects has inspired you and helped you in any way, would you be so kind as to leave a review wherever you purchased this book? That would help me in return. Thanks for reading!

Happy knitting!

Made in the USA
San Bernardino, CA
27 June 2020